AF429784

CONTENTS

CONTENTS

8. Provide Information/Feedback/Document

9. Org Change/HR announcements

10. Introduction

11. Ask for an employment opportunity

CONTENTS

CONTENTS

CONTENTS

1

About This Book

ARE THESE EMAILS REAL?

These emails are excerpts from a database of Enron employee email exchanges. Enron was one of the top U.S. companies in the 1980s and 1990s, but it failed miserably due to an intentional, organized, and creatively planned accounting fraud. Enron's failure raised questions about the accounting practices and activities of many U.S. corporations. Indeed, it led to more standardized and systematic accounting laws and regulations in the U.S.

During the legal investigation into Enron's collapse, the Federal Energy Regulatory Commission (FERC) collected a vast amount of data, including over 600,000 emails generated by 158 employees.

This book is based on a collection of useful expressions and phrases from the actual email exchanges saved within the database.

HOW TO USE THIS BOOK

You can read the whole book and make references later, or you can look up specific events or expressions from the table of contents. In this book, you will find the most commonly used expressions in a business setting. This book includes full sentences where vital terms are printed in boldface. This is done so that you can apply and customize them to communicate more professionally. As stated previously, this book is a reference for creating professional business emails rather than a grammar textbook.

ABOUT THE AUTHOR

Jen works as an analyst at a top U.S. technology company. While completing her higher education here in the U.S. She realized that writing a professional email is significantly different from writing academic papers. She discovered the Enron database during her research project and found many interesting and unique email expressions. Writing a professionally refined email is not an easy task, and she wants to share her resources with anyone going through a similar struggle.

2

Schedule Meetings

INFORMING A MEETING

Thank you all for responding so promptly. **The meeting has been set for** Thursday, April 5, in Portland from 1 PM to approx. 6 PM. Please let me know if I can assist you with any travel plans. I have reserved the Mt. Hood conference room for this meeting.

SETTING UP A MEETING

I am trying to arrange individual 30-minute meetings for Andrea Calo's Houston Trip. She will be available from 2pm to 6pm on Monday. **Would you please let me know if you have any time available to meet with her?** We apologize for the late notice.

Would you like me to schedule a meeting to discuss real time data feeds to customers? If so who should attend?

Let's find a time to discuss this further.

Please let Marde know if you have **a preference as to which day you would like to meet** with Kim.

ATTENDING A MEETING

Please plan on attending a meeting on Thursday, March 23rd at 11am in Room 202. **Please mark your calendar.**

A meeting concerning the above subject is scheduled for 2pm with Stan Horton on Monday. Please try to arrange your schedules to attend, as Stan's schedule is not flexible. **Please confirm your attendance** by email to me by tomorrow, so I can provide Cindy with a headcount.

Attached is an announcement about Board Retreat. We will have dinner and two meetings. **Your attendance is very important** as we will be planning our road map for the next several years. Please RSVP to this email.

RESCHEDULE A MEETING

The staff meeting that is scheduled for tomorrow has been rescheduled to next Friday, May 18th. The meeting is scheduled to start at 2:30 pm central time and will be in EB30C1. If you are not able to attend, please make sure that you send an email to Kim with an explanation.

Unfortunately, due to Jeff's travel schedule, a meeting in January or even early February is not feasible. **I would be happy to schedule a meeting** in late February or early March **if that timing works for you.** Please call me should you wish to proceed on that basis.

I was able to speak with Greg this morning and I regret to inform you that he will not be able to join your class via video conference on April 3rd as we had previously hoped. **Please provide me with some possible future dates** during the month of May and I will discuss them with Greg.

3

Ask for available dates for a meeting

ASK FOR AVAILABLE DATES FOR A MEETING

I have seen a negotiation program that I think worth showing to each of you for your consideration.

I have suggested the 23rd or the 24th of April **as possible dates for a demo**, which would probably be via the Internet. Please let me know your availability for those days.

Mark, I received your voice-mail. Our national Chairman, David Jackson, and I are at your disposal.

Just give us a bit of a **heads-up on timing** and we will come to Houston. Best regards, Dan.

I'm writing on behalf of Jeff Skilling regarding scheduling a 20-minute conference call to discuss the above referenced presentation/panel discussion at the Houston Chapter YPO (Young Presidents Organization) meeting. Jeff is available the afternoon of Thursday, April 12, between the hours of 3:00 p.m. and 5:00 p.m. (CDT). Please let me know **what your availability is during this time period,** and I'll be back in touch to nail down an exact time or to suggest an alternative date/time.

4

Reply to a request/email

GET BACK WITH (TO)

I'll **get back with you** on this within a couple of days.

LATE REPLY

I'm sorry I haven't replied sooner, but there is a decision to be made about what type of product these should fall under. I'll get back to you as soon as we make a decision.

Thanks for the nice note. **Sorry for the delay in getting back to you,** but I took a couple of weeks off for the holidays immediately following the announcement.

Dear Suzanne, **I'm sorry for the delay in returning your e-mail.** We're catching up now after taking some time off over the holidays.

5

Follow-up on meeting/email/ appointment/ deals

FOLLOW-UP ON MEETING/EMAIL/APPOINTMENT/DEALS

Here are the **meeting minutes as I captured them from the meeting** on Tuesday. Please take some time to review and let me know if I missed anything or made any mistakes in my note taking. Thanks for your help.

As a follow-up to my message yesterday, I have talked to George who assured me that he is taking things in India slowly.

I want to follow-up on our discussion yesterday and want to learn more about your company.
Caroline forwarded me your questions regarding the Risk System

so **I wanted to go ahead and respond** since Steve is out this week. Let me know if you have any other questions or there are open issues that we need to address prior to completing the contract.

I'm following up on my email to you of 2/1. David, it's my understanding from our call last week that we do not have any issue. Mary, do you have any comments or concerns from a regulatory standpoint?

Per our phone conversation, here is how to get in touch with me. **I will follow up tomorrow with a quote.** Thanks.

6

Receipt of request

We are in **receipt of your correspondence dated** February 15, 2001. At this time, Mr. Skilling does not wish to schedule an appointment, but he does thank you for the opportunity to review the services you offer. He will contact you should circumstances change.

We are in **receipt of your letter to** Jeff Skilling dated March 30, 2001. Jeff has been traveling for the past 2 weeks; however, I wanted you to know that your letter was received and that you will receive a response as soon as practical.

We are **in receipt of your letter dated** January 26, 2001, **regarding a sponsorship opportunity** at Energy West's Summer Energy Conference. Upon review, we have decided to decline participation.

We are in **receipt of your letter dated** December 6, 2000, addressed to Mr. Jeffrey Skilling **regarding the above opportunity**. Your letter stated that you had also written to Mr. Mark Palmer, among others, at Enron.

7

Ask for Information/ Feedback/ Document

KEEPING SOMEONE INFORMED

Please **keep me in the loop.**
I want to **stay in the loop.**
I will **keep you in the loop.**
Please **keep me updated.**
We will **keep you posted.**
Thank you for **keeping us in the loop on this.** As you suggested,
the intent is to use this data along with other available data to
generate a price for credit. Let's find a time to discuss this further.

ASKING FOR AN UPDATE

**We haven't heard from you for a while and wanted to check
back with you.** If you haven't decided yet, is there anything that
we can do to help you with your decision? Looking forward to
hearing from you soon.

Hi, I'm the commercial person responsible for the sale of the
Alberta PPA. I was **looking for an update on** where this issue is at.
It is my understanding that we need to have an agreement on
the sale of the PPA. What does the prospective timing look like?

Please provide any additional feedback on other issues you would like to talk about. We will be meeting around 12 noon or as soon as they arrive from the airport.

I would greatly appreciate **if you provide me with any feedback on** my performance. I am especially interested in your opinion regarding the areas I need to improve.

Attached is a **draft of the agenda for your review.**

I look forward to your feedback and/or suggestions.
This year I will be putting together the holiday mailing for West Power Trading's customers. **I would like your input as to** what gifts we should send, and how many I should purchase in advance.

ASKING FOR INFO/HELP

We are in need of the following information: Emergency contact name/phone. Please update this information by going through eHRonline or email me with the information. Your cooperation is appreciated!

I would like to get the following information from you. I also realize that it may take some time for you to get the information together: The total volume by month, Monthly production by pipeline. Thank you in advance.

The El Paso model was completely messed up when I came in this evening. I had to change several areas on the second page due to formula errors in mapping the deals over. **I would appreciate it if you could double check it**. I wanted a "second set of eyes."

Bob, Mary and I have been discussing a variety of issues and **need your input** before sending out the invitation, which we should do soon. **Please advise on** the following topics.

ASKING FOR ADVICE

I see that Shemin is out until next week. Since you are becoming a law guru, **you might know the answer to this question.** The following document is an order from the court. Does that mean it has been filed and is in effect now?

ASKING FOR SIGN/PERMISSION

I have received from UBS a confidentiality form which **you are required to sign.** Please either come by my desk to sign or email me your desk location. I would be grateful if you could return these to me by 4 pm, Wed, 6th.

Could you set up the following people with Read and Write access the O:\Research folder. Chris is moving all the information over to the new O: drive. Let me know if you have any questions or concerns.

Please grant full access to all of the west power traders. They had access at one time, but can't get in now.

ASKING FOR RESPONSE

Please respond by next Friday, August 24, so that I may move forward with planning.

ASKING FOR MORE TIME

Thanks for your comprehensive note on your plans. **I want to take a little bit more time to review** this in more detail. I hope that we will have an opportunity to speak in-person sometime in the not too distant future.

8

Provide Information/ Feedback/ Document

PROVIDING AN UPDATE

I want to provide you with an update. I know how frustrating these times are for everyone. I appreciate your continuing patience.

I would give you a quick update on our conversations regarding Atlantic Copper. Our team met with the senior management from Atlantic Copper last week in concert with the London Metal Exchange Week.

DIRECTING ALL QUESTIONS

Please be aware that remote connectivity into the Enron network has changed. Authorization to use eConnect may be requested via the eRequest system. **Please direct all questions or concerns to the** Resolution Center at xxx.

SUGGESTING HELP

Mark, attached is a Business Review format **which may (or may not) be helpful for** your Business Review Meeting. Please take a look and see what you think. Let me know.

Please let me know **if I can assist you** with any travel plans.

SHARING ONE'S THOUGHT

I think we are on the right track from our meeting. **My thought is that** we get a good working model and take it back to our groups. **We can see** how it works and determine what we need to tinker with

Please let me know **if I can assist you** with any travel plans.

SHARING FEEDBACK

I wanted to give you some great feedback I got on Janelle's hedging presentation at the NARUC conference. Herb Tate, a former NJ commissioner, said that Janelle "knocked them dead." Herb is now serving as the FERC judge's consultant for the "one" Southeast RTO mediation for the next month.

PROVIDING DOCUMENTS

Per your request, **attached are the documents.**

Attached are the documents **you have requested.**

Tracy and Dan, Steve and I revised the business development slides for Stan's presentation.

I'm waiting for Kim to update the TransPecos slide and **will forward** final version **when completed, probably on Monday.**

Attached is the final draft of the deal. I will be scheduling a plant tour and meeting with the appropriate folks to pin down logistics and communication protocols. Please give me a call if you'd like to discuss.

9

Org Change/HR announcements

ANNOUNCING PROMOTION

We are pleased to announce the following mid-year promotions. Typically, we do few to no mid-year promotions, but given the accomplishments of this office over the last few years and the individual contributions that have led to our success, we feel that **these are both well-deserved and appropriate. Please join us in congratulating the following individuals who were promoted from** Manager **to** Director.

POSITION CHANGE

I want to give all of you an update to my previous message on the replacement for Brian in Finance. **Jennifer was going to be his replacement;** however, Jennifer has accepted a position in Energy. **The newest addition to Finance** is Holly who joins us from Bank United. Brian will be helping to transition Holly into her new responsibilities. Please join me in welcoming Jennifer and Holly into her new role.

As a follow-up to the Enron All Employee meeting, **we are pleased to announce** several org changes. Jeff Johnson will **move into the new role** of CIO … Anthony Dayao will continue as CIO for EES Systems … John Paskin will transfer to the Houston office from London … Beth Perlman will **work closely with** Mark on key projects … **Replacing** Beth in **her current role will be** Steve Hotte …

I want to let you know that **I really enjoyed working with you.** It has been a pleasure to work for such great people. I hope **to stay in contact with you**. Thanks again.

I regret to inform you that Ken has decided to leave Enron to pursue other opportunities. I am grateful to him for his outstanding service to Enron. **Please join me wishing him the best in his new endeavors.**

I wanted to **give you the courtesy of hearing directly from me that I submitted my resignation.** My departure date is still open for discussion, and I will do my best to make the most complete and successful transition as possible for Enron and myself.

It has been my pleasure to work with you all in my wonderful years at Enron. I will be leaving Enron today. I will you all continued success. Please feel free to contact me at …

I am going to be the Senior Regulatory Counsel at ISO New England starting on April 9, 2001. **My last day in the Portland area will be** March 31. **I enjoyed working with you and wish you the best of everything.** My new address will be:

Effective April 6, 2001, **I am resigning my position as** Director of Federal Regulatory Affairs. It has been a pleasure working with you. I will be working today and will be on vacation for the remainder of the time. During my vacation, I can be reached at home at xx

Congratulations Mary. I've enjoyed working with you over the years, and **look forward to seeing you in your new role.** Mary, **Good luck to you and I hope our path's cross again!** I'm glad we worked together enough for me to get to know you! And if I can be of assistance (either formally, or informally) feel free to let me know.

We regret to announce that Amy Fitzpatrick will be leaving Enron's Portland office in September. Amy's husband, Simon, has accepted a job in New Jersey, and it didn't make sense for them to "commute" coast to coast. Amy will continue to work here for the next month or two **to hire her replacement and to make sure that her responsibilities have been completely handed over.** We really appreciate having such long lead time to effectuate this transition.

Amy **has made tremendous contributions to our office** over the last 14 months. We really appreciate her efforts. We realize that Amy has become integral to the efficient operation of the Portland office and **want to make her transition as smooth as possible.** If you have any concerns or wish to get any issues on to the "transition list" please let your manager and/or Amy know.

HIRING A NEW PERSON

He is a strong candidate. Well rounded, excellent leadership experience, very personable, confident, and sold himself well. He may have outstanding offers from other firms.

I would like to have an analyst start as soon as possible. I had already talked to Mason before, but he opted for another rotation. So, let me know what the procedure is and when I could expect an analyst. Thanks.

Elizabeth is currently working as a contract employee for Sherry. She told me her contract runs out at the end of this month. Tim and I both loved working with her and think she **would be a good employee to keep if you have any spots available.**

I see job #1154 on the job posting board. **I am going to apply for it online.** I thought you said that there are two open positions. Do you know if it has been posted yet or are you using job #1154 to fill both positions?

RECOMMENDING A PERSON

Brent Dornier is an analyst who is moving back to Houston from London. He has been invited to join the trading track program and was scheduled to spend the first rotation on the west desk. **I met him face to face** in London a few weeks ago and think **he is exceptionally strong.**

Cindy is the Executive VP for HR at Enron Corp **who I have observed operate in several contexts.** At Ken Lay's request, she ran the Governor's Business Council while I was GC and has been an active and effective spokesperson for Enron. She is now one of his top executives.

I have a friend who is interested in an HR position with Enron. She spoke of a rotational program for HR that I am not familiar with. Do you know anything about the program, or who I might forward her resume to for an HR related position in general. She has a few years of experience with a smaller firm, and I think she's looking for a company with a more established HR department like Enron. Also, **do you have knowledge of specific positions we are trying to fill** in ENA? Any info would be helpful. Thanks.

ADVERTISING A JOB/POSITION

We are searching for an individual to join the west gas trading desk on a temporary basis to lead the development of a comprehensive energy model. Mike Roberts **suggested** that a member from your research team **might be a good fit.** I am very excited by the scope and depth that can be achieved with your help. Please let me know if you are interested.

The Analyst and Associate Programs recognize we have many **Analyst needs that need to be addressed immediately.** While we anticipate many new Analysts joining Enron this summer (late May) and fulltime (August) we felt it necessary to address some of the immediate needs with an Off-Cycle Recruiting event. We are planning this event for Thursday, February 15 and are **inviting approximately 30 candidates to be interviewed.**

I am asking that you **forward this note to any potential interviewers** (Managers or above). We will conduct first round interviews in the morning and the second round interviews in the afternoon.

EXTENDING AN OFFER

I would like to extend an offer to Cynthia. I interviewed her last week. If you have any question, please let me know or contact Patti @x30494. Thanks for your help.

ACCEPTING AN OFFER

Just to update my previous memo, Cynthia has **just accepted our offer, with a tentative start date of** Monday, July 17th.

NEW HIRE

I am delighted that you will be joining us in September. We look forward to working with you.

10

Introduction

INTRODUCING ONESELF FOR A POSITION

Judy Lay Allen, an associate of yours on the Federal Reserve board, spoke with Joannie Williamson today regarding my desire to interview at Enron.

I am a graduate of Princeton University with two years experience in financial modeling and communications. Towards assessing my skill set relative to peers, I took and received a 740 on my GMAT. I have also interned in a gas exploration company and am familiar with the industry; likewise, I have worked with clients in telecommunications and am aware of the work Enron is doing in the bandwidth trading/pooling field.

I am aware of Enron's executive training/business analyst programs and **am highly interested in exploring opportunities** therein. I am in Houston through Friday evening and, given the short notice, would be grateful for **any opportunity to meet with the appropriate person** any time Thursday or Friday.

I look forward to interviewing and applying my experience at Enron.

INTRODUCING A PERSON FOR A POSITION

Cindy is the Executive VP for HR at Enron Corp who I have observed operate in several contexts. At Ken Lay's request, she ran the Governor's Business Council while I was GC and has been an active and effective spokesperson for Enron. She is now one of his top executives.

She is **a top quality "all around athlete."** Ken called me this morning to tell me that Cindy had **expressed a high interest and capacity to work for** you in the transition. I know you are getting many calls of this sort, but this is one you may want to look at. She's attractive, articulate, experienced, a great team player, energetic and a focused worker.

Ken is going to send her resume to me, **I will forward her resume to you** as soon as I have it.

Sanjay, Jeff **asked me to write you to introduce you** to Gerald Chan, the brother of Ronnie Chan (ENE director). Gerald has been investing in capital ventures in the US and Asia for many years. Of late, he has been running into companies in which Enron is investing or is interested in investing, and Jeff met with him today to discuss this. Jeff suggested that Gerald **contact you to discuss further.** I have provided Gerald with your telephone numbers, address and e-mail address. You should expect to hear from him shortly.

For your information, below is the pertinent information on Gerald: Neither Mike nor I have interviewed Scott before. Our connection to Scott **came through a very strong recommendation from** our West-Power trading desk. We are interested in Scott because his **experience is directly related to** the west gas market that Mike and I trade. I don't mean to be a pain. If this is unconventional, Mike and I will make separate arrangements for Scott to meet with us.

I am pleased to announce that effectively immediately Stan Horton **will assume leadership responsibility** as chairman and CEO of Enron Global Assets, which will continue to report to John. **Please join me in supporting** Stan in his new role.

It is my pleasure to announce that Ken **has joined** Enron Energy Corp. He **will be reporting directly to** Don and will support Central America. Ken has over 25-year experience in gas industry and has been working for Enron since 1996.

11

Ask for an employment opportunity

ASK FOR AN EMPLOYMENT OPPORTUNITY

I once again want to highlight that if **I am given a chance, I will do all I can to prove that the people who gave me this chance made the right decision.**

I am interested in employment opportunities with your company. I have a proven record of success and look forward to new challenges. I have attached my resume which details my experience and capabilities.

Lisa Jones in the Analyst program said that you have an opening for an analyst and **I was wondering if that position had been filled.** I've attached my resume. Thanks.

I am very excited about the opportunity and **I am looking forward to becoming a valuable asset** to Real Time and Enron as a whole. I am confident the position would be an excellent fit.

12

Business Deal/ Contract/ Partnership

BUSINESS DEAL/CONTRACT/PARTNERSHIP

Steve, congrats on the closure of the Alamac deal! It certainly was a lengthy process/negotiation, but well worth it. Thanks for jumping in like you did in the beginning, your focus and effort really made a difference. Hopefully, we'll work together again soon!

I need to **review the contract with** Rob and we will have **some minor adjustments to make.** I will set up a meeting when we are ready. It will be probably towards the end of next week.

I got your name and email address from Chad and was hoping **to arrange a time to briefly (and informally) talk to you** about our B2B business and whether you think there might be **any opportunities for some strategic partnership.**

As per our conversation today, I am sending you **an outline of what we intend to be doing.** I have included a business plan to show the scope of the opportunity. Let me know if you have any further questions.

I reached out to Franco, and he returned my call. He mentioned that IMI (the Italian investment bank) would **like to do a joint-venture with us** to develop a power trading structure. He will put me in contact with someone at IMI. You can reach him at any of the above numbers.

Attached **please find the current draft of the contract.** Please let me know how you would like to proceed. As I mentioned, **we are trying to finalized the contract very shortly.** I look forward to working with you on this matter.

13

Seeking agreement

Do we need to discuss this further? I just want to be o**n the same page.** Let me know what you think.

Keith, I've just spoke with Mark, and he agrees with all this. If you want to give me a call when you have a minute, I'll conference in Mark, and **we'll just confirm all this.**

14

Committee/
Volunteer

Thank you for agreeing to **serve on the Committee.** This initial meeting will be a brainstorming session to try to develop more proactive ideas to ask for contributions to the Be A Resource Program to purchase bikes and scooters for the children for Christmas.

VOLUNTEER

Please take a moment to review the attached document that has been sent into the coordinator of the CFSA Tournament volunteers. As you will see **we are still in need of** a volunteer list from most of you. For those of you who have turned in your list, thank you very much, **your prompt attention to this request is greatly appreciated.**

15

Alternative/ Replacement

ALTERNATIVE/REPLACEMENT

I am disappointed that Joe will not be able to join us at our next Advisory Council meeting. However Tom **sounds like an excellent alternative.** Would you please contact him and see if he might be willing to join us for the next meeting and talk about the subjects you suggested.

I want to give all of you an update to my previous message on the replacement for Brian in Finance. **Jennifer was going to be his replacement;** however, Jennifer has accepted a position in Energy.

This is unfortunately true. Rod and Steve have been involved in this. At this point in time, **there is not a better alternative.**

Please let me know what your availability is during this time period, and I'll be back in touch to nail down an exact time or to **suggest an alternative date/time.**

16

Bring to attention

John, below are several issues **I wanted to bring to your attention** prior to finalizing merit increases for East Power. I have also given David Oxley the same information in order for you to discuss this morning when you meet. Call me if you have any questions.

Thanks for the heads up, Michael. We're working to track down the source and remove it. We really appreciate **you bringing it to our attention**.

Thank you for **your prompt attention** to this matter.

17

Handle an issue

I did receive your e-mails and wanted to assure you that **your concerns are being dealt with.**

Looks like **we've gotten to the bottom of this billing issue.** The IT group is going to refund you $360.00 for erroneous charges over the last year. I have them audit your bill, and this is the amount you are due.

In an effort to **handle these matters in an efficient and coordinated manner,** we have assigned Geoff as the Enron point person. I am forwarding your request to him. Geoff can be reached at 713-853-7058. Please let me know if I can help in any way.

Please disregard the list from my previous email. The following list contains the CORRECT contact information for our candidates. **I apologize for the inconvenience.**

18

Congratulations/
Acknowledgement

Congratulations on your promotion to Director. It is **well deserved and most appropriate.** They couldn't have found a better person.

I would like to acknowledge David Portz for his hard work and diligence in drafting and actively supporting the negotiation of the deal. David worked long hours ensuring all tight timelines were met and facilitated quick contract turnarounds on numerous occasions.

19

Thank You Emails

Bill,

Thanks very much for taking the time to speak with me this afternoon. I am very interested in a real-time trading position in Portland. It sounds like an excellent opportunity and a challenge that I am ready to take on. I have heard many good things about the group in Portland and I trust that real-time trading would be an exceptional learning experience. I certainly look forward to visiting Portland and further discussing this opportunity with you and your team.

Your e-mail was such a pleasant surprise! **Thanks so much for the kind words.**

I would love to get together for lunch in the near future, though January is typically a tough month for me. I'll have my assistant, Sherri Sera, call your office to see what we can arrange.

Thanks again for the note. I look forward to seeing you soon.

20

Apology

I am very sorry, but I inadvertently deleted your e-mail before printing the attachment for Mr. Lay. Will you please send it again? Thanks.

Hey there! **Sorry this response is so late!** I read your email on a night when I was really busy and then just kind of spaced out in replying back. I got your pictures and the card. Thanks a bunch! I gotta run now but talk to you later!

Phillip, **I apologize that** it has taken me so long to send you an e-mail like you asked us to, but I just wanted to send some suggestions/ thoughts about things on the East Desk. I really like the idea of weekly meetings. Especially in the new building where we will be spaced out and not all sitting together, I think it would be good for team unity.

I needed to apologize for my inability to handle myself in more of a professional manner. I thought I had moved on from being an emotional basket case, but as we found out, I haven't. Again, **please accept my apology.** I just need to move forward and stop reflecting on the past. It is so difficult when you have given your entire career for an organization that still doesn't see value in you. But, that is my problem not yours.

21

On behalf of

I'm **writing on behalf of Jeff Skilling** in response to your note below. Jeff would be delighted to join you for lunch on your visit to Houston. In looking at this schedule, he is currently available for lunch on the following dates: May 16, 19, 24, 25

Please let us know which, if any, of these dates work best for you. **On behalf of** Jeff Skilling, thank you very much for the invitation to speak to the San Diego Chapter of YPO. Jeff was very flattered and somewhat intrigued by your offer. However, given the current demands on his time, he must respectfully decline your invitation. Please let me know if you have any interest in another senior-level representative of Enron speaking to your group, and I'll be happy to do what I can to facilitate that for you.

If you can attend this meeting **on my behalf,** I'd appreciate it. With such short notice, no problem if you can't. I'll be in the office tomorrow morning, barring weather travel problems.

22

Vacation/Out of Office message

I will be **out of the office for the next two weeks and will be returning on** Jan. 2nd, 2001. Dana will be here to help you while I am away.

I will **be on vacation beginning** Oct 4th, **returning on** Oct 10th. I can be reached via email or phone (xxx-xxx-xxxx). **In case of emergency**, please contact Gary at xxx-xxx-xxxx

OUT OF OFFICE NOTIFICATION

If you are going to be out of the office, please have your assistant send me an e-mail with the dates you will be out and the telephone number where you can be contacted. Thank you.

REQUESTING VACATION

Yesterday I mentioned that **I would like to take some unused vacation** before I move to Cara's group. I was hoping to get off August 10-19, and was hoping to be scheduled for the day shift on Aug. 9 (so I can catch an evening flight). Please let me know if this is OK with you. I'm copying Slinger.

23

Personal Emails

HOW ARE YOU DOING?

How are you doing? **I haven't heard from you in a while.** I would love to **get together sometime.** My phone number is xxx. Call me when you can.

DINNER INVITATION

Micheal Holthouse and Matt Khourie (Jeff's co-hosts of the April 24 YPO event) invite you to join them at dinner on Monday evening, April 23. Reservations have been made in Matt Khourie's name at Capital Grille, located at 5365 Westheimer Road (in the Galleria area), at 7:00 p.m. Should you need transportation to the restaurant, I will be happy to make those arrangements for you. **Please send me a note confirming your attendance** at this dinner. I look forward to hearing from you.

GOOD LUCK

I have been following the latest development of your firm. **Hope everything turns out well in the end.** Would be fun to meet up for a drink some time. I'm in Houston on a regular basis. Hope all is well.

Hi Mark. I know that you are busy with critical Enron business matters now. I don't want to intrude on your time at this critical juncture. I **do want to wish you much luck and success** in getting things worked out.

I know how frustrating these times are for everyone. **I appreciate your continuing patience.**

24

Other useful expressions

AT YOUR LEISURE

I will maintain this spreadsheet, and you're encouraged to reference it **at your leisure.** Please let me know if you have questions.

BOOKED SOLID

Edward, Jeff is **booked solid** today and Friday and traveling tomorrow. He then will be on vacation from December 18-January 2. I would suggest that you send him an e-mail. If he needs any additional information, we can try to get the two of you together for a few minutes the morning of the interview.

CATCH BY SURPRISE

I am micro-managing this deal and I don't want it **to catch you by surprise.** Do you want me to update the spreadsheet? I need to know by tomorrow morning. Thanks.

DEADLINE IN JEOPARDY

Please review the comments below. Unfortunately, there are some issues that have not been resolved and may be **putting our deadline in jeopardy.**

DISTRIBUTION LIST

Have you published the final report yet? If so, I was not on the **distribution list.** Also, could you forward me the link?

DON'T HAVE SPECIFICS (OR DETAILS)

As of yet : same as "as yet" or "yet"

Hello, everyone! I have some sad news to report. Stan's father, Eugene S. Horton, passed away yesterday. **I don't know all the specifics on** what happened, and I don't have the specifics on the funeral arrangements **as of yet;**

DOUBLE CHECK

Second set of eyes : Another person to examine or critique something.

I would appreciate **it if you could double check it**. I wanted a **"second set of eyes."**

EXTEND AN INVITATION

We are excited to **extend an invitation** to you to participate in Pilot 3 of Enron's new ClickAtHome program.

FREE UP TIME

Jeff's time is committed through February 2002, so knowing what the dates/timeframes are would be most helpful in the event we need to try to **free up some time**. Thank you.

FRIENDLY REMINDER

Just a **friendly reminder** that when returning in travel receipts, please indicate what meeting was attended, as well as the names of all guests written on the meal receipts.

GET A CHANCE

We just talked on the phone and I work with Ruth on the Enron Estate Team. Please call me at xxx.xxx.xxxx **when you get a chance.**

GET UP TO SPEED

Mark, I would encourage you to come down to 29 (assuming you are on 33) and we will be more than happy to share all our resources to **get you up to speed** in our analysis.

HAVEN'T HAD A CHANCE YET

I haven't had a chance to send it yet. Paul is out of office today, so I haven't had a chance to talk to him.

IN THE PROCESS OF

I am **in the process of** making the arrangements for a new hire dinner, to take place on Thursday, April 26th (possibly on Wed, April 25th). Could you please let me know if you will be available to attend? Dinner will most likely be around 6pm at either the Heathman, or Oritalia at the Westin.

IN ORDER TO

Bill, I would really like to sign up for the derivatives course being offered on June 4th. I had already requested the 1st thru the 5th off **in order to** attend a wedding in LA, however, I would like to attend the course and I would cut my trip short if selected. Let me know. Thank you.

INADVERTENTLY: without intention; accidentally

I am very sorry, but I **inadvertently** deleted your e-mail before printing the attachment for Mr. Lay. Will you please send it again?

LEAVE UP TO

I talked to Mike Moran this morning and he suggested you for participation in this corporate working group (see below). Very glad to have you. Other group members are from various parts of Public Affairs, both U.S. and International. Mike also said you may want to have Maria Pavlou participate, which I **leave up to you.** The perspective from the pipeline group will be a great addition to our effort.

LIVING DOCUMENT : A living document, also known as an evergreen document or dynamic document, is a document that is continually edited and updated.

Attached, for your information, is a copy of a general presentation that I prepared to illustrate and describe EGM's businesses. This is a presentation that will become a "living" document to communicate our businesses and growth. I will be making numerous changes as we move closer to the analyst meeting in January but I wanted to give everyone a copy of this version.

ON THE RIGHT TRACK

I think **we are on the right track** from our meeting.

SAME PAGE

To ensure **we are all on the same page,** I would like to set up a meeting.

OPEN FOR DISCUSSION

I wanted to give you the courtesy of hearing directly from me that I submitted my resignation. **My departure date is still open for discussion,** and I will do my best to make the most complete and successful transition as possible for Enron and myself.

PLEASANT SURPRISE

Your e-mail was **such a pleasant surprise**! Thanks so much for the kind words.

POINT OF CONTACT

Is there **a single point of contact** on your team focused on bankruptcy claims? We have had an increase in claims as of late and I am having trouble tracking down the current status on each case. Let me know if you can help. Thanks.

PROSPECTIVE TIMING

Hi, I'm the commercial person responsible for the sale of the Alberta PPA. I was looking for an update on where this issue is at. It is my understanding that we need to have an agreement on the sale of the PPA. What does the **prospective timing** look like?

RUN BY

Attached is a draft of the agenda for your review. I had an opportunity to **run it by** Jeff last week. He was happy with the theme and the first day's schedule.

In the meantime, **I'll run this by Jeff** to see if he thinks it makes sense. Do you have any dates for future dinners in mind? The vast majority of

SERIOUS CONSIDERATION

Apologies for the delay in responding to your e-mail below.

Jeff has given your proposal **serious consideration.** However, given the current demands on his time, he has decided to decline your offer to join the Cogent Communications Advisory Committee.

On behalf of Jeff, many thanks for the opportunity and best wishes for success.

SHORT NOTICE

Greg will have to leave Houston for some of our overseas offices beginning April 2nd for approx. two weeks (London, Tokyo & Sydney). I do apologize **for the short notice,** but these things tend to happen quickly, and with little or no notice.

| SOLICIT FEEDBACK, JOINT EFFORT: something done by two or more people or groups working together.

Again, this is Maria's view of the situation, which might be totally different from your team's perspective. We do not want the situation to become an "us v. them" mentality, so I am taking this opportunity to **solicit your feedback.** Dennis and I are hoping we can work diligently to make up this time and resolve these issues in a **joint effort.** We look forward to your comments and completing this link once and for all.

| STOP BY

Kim would like to **stop by** the office to do some TTT training next Wed, Thurs or Fri.

| TAKE THE LIBERTY OF : venture to do something without first asking permission.

Thank you for your recent correspondence to Mr. Jeff Skilling. As he is traveling for the next 10 days, I have **taken the liberty of** forwarding your information to Mr. Greg Piper, COO of Enron Net Works. Mr. Piper is responsible for all of Enron's e-commerce systems development.

TAKING A HARD LOOK: to think carefully about something, especially with the result that you change your opinions or behavior

Enron Europe is **taking a hard look at** all the allocations they receive from Corp. Can you send me a note providing details on your budget allocation methodology? I've attached your spreadsheet in case you need it for reference.

TENTATIVELY

Ann is unavailable to interview next week. I have **tentatively scheduled her interview for** Monday, April 16th, at 10:00am in Mt. Hood. As Amy already has an interview at 10:00am, Bill will interview first.

TIGHT TIMELINES

I would like to acknowledge David Portz for his hard work and diligence in drafting and actively supporting the negotiation of the deal. David worked long hours **ensuring all tight timelines were met** and facilitated quick contract turnarounds on numerous occasions.

TOUCH BASE WITH

I want to touch **base with you** to see how your DealBench experience is going. I am happy to walk through the functionality within the site. I look forward to hearing from you.

UNDER THE IMPRESSION

I was **under the impression** that what you and I had worked out was more of a temporary fix and that there was another group working on a permanent solution for all of us.

UNFORTUNATELY

This is **unfortunately true.** Rod and Steve have been involved in this. At this point in time, there is not a better alternative.

Susie, **unfortunately I will be unable to attend** these classes due to a scheduling conflict with my new position. However, if you could let me know when the next class is it would be greatly appreciated.

UNTIL FURTHER NOTICE

We have not heard back from Carla about her jury duty and whether it will continue through tomorrow. Therefore could you inform your group to continue sending the deal correction emails to me **until further notice?** Thank you for your attention to this matter.

URGENT NEED

We are in **urgent need of** approximately 35 interviewers for this weekend's Super Saturday recruiting, to which 105 analyst and associate candidates have been invited. You all realize the importance of these efforts, and I would appreciate you encouraging members of your organization to participate this weekend.

www.ingramcontent.com/pod-product-compliance
Lightning Source LLC
Chambersburg PA
CBHW070917160726
48004CB00003B/1407